Su
Biblical

Hats off to Phil Moser for helping us navigate through life's most challenging issues in a clearly biblical way. The thing I like about these booklets is that they are forged by a pastor who has successfully wrestled through these issues with his flock, and thankfully he now shares these insights with the church at large.

DR. JOSEPH M. STOWELL, PRESIDENT,
CORNERSTONE UNIVERSITY, GRAND RAPIDS, MICHIGAN

Pastors often face a variety of problems in their weekly counseling. Every issue that requires counseling flows from some kind of sinful behavior—either a sin of commission or omission. Despite the multifaceted nature of sin and its consequences, these problems all stem from a single source; the love of self over the love of Christ. Because of this singular source, there are foundational spiritual principles that can be applied to every situation to call men and women back to the love of Christ first and foremost. In this easy to understand booklet, Phil Moser has done an admirable job of identifying those principles and then applying them to daily life. I commend this work both to those who are struggling in their daily walk, and to those counselors who are seeking additional tools to sharpen their counseling.

DR. JOHN MACARTHUR, PASTOR-TEACHER
GRACE COMMUNITY CHURCH
HEARD ON GRACE TO YOU

The life that Jesus lived often seems out of reach and distant from our suburban world. In <u>Just Like Jesus</u>, Phil Moser lays out a clear and biblical strategy for spiritual growth and progress. This book should really carry a warning label, "Caution: grows passionate believers."

DON LOUGH, JR., EXECUTIVE DIRECTOR,
WORD OF LIFE FELLOWSHIP
SCHROON LAKE, NEW YORK

Pastor Moser's writing reflects a deep commitment to helping individuals both understand and obey God's Word in their daily life. As an experienced counselor he realizes that just teaching the truth is not enough; people need help on the practical steps of disciplining themselves for the purpose of godliness. I commend his combination of exposition, call to obedience and "how-to."

RANDY PATTEN, EXECUTIVE DIRECTOR,
NATIONAL ASSOCIATION OF NOUTHETIC COUNSELORS

I am delighted to commend the work of Pastor Phil Moser whose Biblical Strategies ministry builds on the person of the Lord Jesus Christ and the power of God's Word.

RICHARD MAYHUE, TH.D.,
EXECUTIVE VICE PRESIDENT AND DEAN
THE MASTERS' SEMINARY, SUN VALLEY, CA

Just Like Jesus

biblical strategies for growing well

Phil Moser

Just Like Jesus: biblical strategies for growing well

Published and Distributed by Biblical Strategies.

Visit our Web site: www.biblicalstrategies.com

© 2012 Phil Moser
International Standard Book Number: 978-0-9881942-0-5

Credits:
Cover Art: gracewaymedia.com, Gary Lizzi
Copy Editors: Wes Brown, Jennifer Kraft, Barb Lawton
Logo Design: Samurai Virtual Tours
Website Design: Samurai Virtual Tours

CONTENTS

JUST LIKE JESUS

MARY fought back the fear rising in her chest. She could feel the muscles in her back tightening uncontrollably. Frightened, she tried to recite the verses she had learned as a child. The contraction subsided, and she rested. There was cause for the fear she felt. Having never known a man, she was about to give birth to a son.

Joseph's deep voice began to hum a familiar melody. It was just like him to hum only the tune so she would have to voice the lyric. Between contractions, she quietly sang along to the song she had written months earlier:

How my soul praises the Lord. How my spirit rejoiced in God my Savior! For he took notice of his lowly servant girl, and from now on all generations will call me blessed.[1]

But Mary's sweet song was driven from her mind with God's promise to Eve, "I will sharpen the pain of your pregnancy, and in pain you will give birth."[2]

The final contraction was the worst. The young girl's body stretched between time and eternity. Satan was insistent upon the child's destruction, but the Father's desires would be accomplished precisely on time.[3] Mary pushed hard and heard her newborn son's first cry. His tiny lungs inhaled earth's air as a human being. Amidst the chaotic noise of an overcrowded Bethlehem night, she heard her husband's gentle voice, "We will call Him Jesus, for He will save His people from their sins."[4]

Years later, the apostle John would capture this event with nine simple words: "And the Word became flesh, and dwelt among us."[5]

J ESUS Christ, although fully God, was born fully human. If you embrace this truth, you will desire to follow his example. If you do not, living *just like* Jesus will seem beyond your reach. You might even wonder if it's possible. After all, you might reason, "He is God and I am not."

Yet, the Scriptures don't let us off the hook so easily. John, who defended both the humanity[6] and deity[7] of Jesus, charged us to live just like Jesus. He wrote, "Whoever says he abides in him ought to walk in the same way in which he walked."[8]

When I study the deity of Christ, I am drawn to worship him, but when I study the humanity of Christ, I am inspired to live like him. The first causes me to realize what I am not, but the latter causes me to realize what I should be. When I confuse the two, I no longer see my need to depend fully on the resources Jesus used because I assume he used a resource unavailable to me—his deity.

Several years ago, I had two conversations that confirmed the importance of applying the humanity of Christ to the Christian life. The first was with my ten-year-old daughter; the second was with a man in his forties. Both individuals were different in every way, and both were struggling with different temptations. Yet when I encouraged them to walk just like Jesus, they gave the same answer: *I'm not Jesus. Jesus is God. I am not.* Both overlooked the simple fact that Jesus became man.

Here is a significant, yet forgotten truth behind the incarnation of Christ: Jesus walked where you walk so that you might learn to walk like he walked. Jesus communicates this truth further when he repeatedly uses the phrase "follow me."[9] Your thoughts, feelings, and choices should be modeled after him. No matter your age, growing well means learning to walk *just like Jesus.*

Could it be that you, like me, have spent your entire life thinking about the ways you are different from Jesus, when he became fully human to show you the ways you could be like him? Have you emphasized his deity at the expense of his humanity? Have you considered the primary means by which Jesus battled temptation as a man? If his victory over temptation was possible, is yours?

This isn't an abstract theological idea; this is a life-changing truth. If Jesus was fully human as the Bible declares, then he lived out his entire earthly life under the intrinsic limitations of humanity.[10] His victory over temptation was possible through his reliance upon resources that are available to you and me today. Let that thought settle in. Jesus did not reach outside his human limitations when being tempted to sin. Instead, he operated within the confines of his humanity when he battled temptation. That's what it means to be tempted like we are, yet without sin.[11]

Embracing Jesus' full humanity[12] is one of the most significant "how" factors for living the Christian life. Practically speaking, once you are in Christ, your victory will not come as a result of the latest trend, program, or motivational speaker. Your growth and change will take place only as you learn to avail yourself of the same resources that Jesus depended upon. What are those resources? How did Jesus acquire them, and what do you and I need to do to become proficient in their use?

THE FIRST RESOURCE: PRAYER

J ESUS was tired—really tired. His ministry had accelerated at a feverish pace. The crowds were large now; and even though the lines were long, the people stayed to see him. They pressed upon him without reprieve. Jesus was physically drained and emotionally spent, yet he kept responding to their desperate cries for help. After all, it was for this reason he had come. As the day grew late, Jesus succumbed to his exhaustion and slept. He was so tired that no one could awaken him. The crowds left; his disciples collapsed from their weariness.

In the early morning darkness, Jesus' eyes snapped open. Instantly, he was wide awake.[13] The gentle snoring of his followers reminded his muscles of their weariness, but his spirit was restless. It refused to let him sleep. He recognized the sense of urgency. It came more regularly now. He craved prayer.

He smiled as he slipped quietly from his place on the floor, careful not to disturb his friends. His pulse quickened as he stepped outside into the cool darkness. He could not wait to speak to his Father. Jesus was learning quickly, and there was so much to share.

For as long as he could remember, he had prayed, and he was still growing in his practice of it. When he was younger, he had prayed out of simple obedience; but as he had matured, he found prayer to be an irreplaceable resource. He needed it. He wanted it. He could not survive without it. Like the runner whose trained body needed exercise, his spirit deeply desired prayer. If only he could find a solitary place . . .[14]

Y OU can read all that Jesus said on prayer in a few minutes. In twice that time, you can read all the Gospel
accounts of Jesus praying. However, you will never tap the
God-given resource of meaningful prayer in that amount of
time. You will need to put in the hours that Jesus did as he
learned to pray.

When you read the biblical accounts, it seems like
Jesus desired to pray most when his life was the busiest.[15]
Those opening days of ministry were fast paced. Jesus
healed many.[16] Demons scattered right and left, forced to
acknowledge his sovereign power over them.[17] Wherever
Jesus spoke, he gathered crowds, and all were amazed at
the authority of his teaching.[18]

Mark communicates this feverish pace through the
word "immediately." He uses it 42 times in his gospel record – seven times in the first chapter alone.[19] So much
happens so fast that you can almost get tired just reading
it! On one of those mornings after a full day of ministry,
Peter was the first disciple to wake. A fisherman by trade,
his weathered body recovered rapidly from fatigue. Ministry was waiting, and people were gathering, but where was
Jesus?

At this juncture Mark's gospel gives us our first
glimpse into how Jesus *practiced* prayer. He writes, "Now in
the morning, having risen a long while before daylight, He
went out and departed to a solitary place; and there He
prayed."[20] While the disciples were trying to keep up with
the demands of the crowd, Jesus was not. His commitment
to prayer moved everything else to second place, and his
schedule confirmed it.

J. Oswald Sanders saw it the same way. He wrote,
"Mastering the art of prayer, like any art, will take time,
and the amount of time we allocate to it will be the true

measure of our conception of its importance."[21] Sanders served as the director of the China Inland Mission for more than two decades. During his lifetime he published 40 books. His speaking schedule was packed. A gracious man, he was in demand his entire life. I heard him speak when he was 91 years old. He shuffled to the platform with the assistance of two men. They placed his hands on the lectern; he grasped it for stability, and began to speak. While age had slowed his body, it had not altered his schedule. Just like Jesus, Sanders understood, *the more you are needed, the more you need to pray.*

Perhaps your life is filled with demands. When your schedule is full and life is fast, prayer is often the first thing to go. Not so with Jesus. He made prayer his top priority; he prayed *before* working.[22]

JESUS AND THE PRACTICE OF PRAYER

Jesus' prayer life provides an excellent example of the way we should pray. He had a specific plan, place, and purpose in prayer. These are essential if we intend to pray like him.

A Specific Plan: He Prayed Early in the Morning

Jesus prayed "early in the morning."[23] Perhaps your first thought of the morning is how much you have to do that day. Email is loading up on your phone before you even get out of bed. Your part-time job feels like a full-time job. Kids' music lessons and sports schedules consume your non-work hours. You volunteer at church and meet in a small group during the week. Before long, prayer is crowded out.

Jesus refused to let prayer take second place. He wasn't alone in this practice. Consider these Old Testament believers: Moses,[24] Job,[25] and Ezra.[26] Even with full schedules, they made time for God "early in the morning." Whatever time you choose to pray, it must be a priority. In a tightly scheduled lifestyle, if prayer is the last thing you plan on doing, chances are it won't get done.

A Specific Place: He Departed to a Solitary Location

Jesus was looking for a *solitary* place.[27] The Greek word translated "solitary" can also mean *uninhabited*.[28] Jesus was not known for being aloof. He loved people, enjoyed being with them, and was at ease in groups of all sizes. Yet, when he prayed, he sought to be alone.

We would do well to follow Jesus' practice. When we pray, we need a location where we will not be interrupted. No cell phones. No texting. No Facebook. Give your conversation with God your undivided attention.

Even when you find a quiet location, your busy mind may still make solitude a challenge. You will need to consciously labor at controlling your thoughts.[29] At times, I have taken a notebook so that if an unfinished task comes to mind, I can simply write it down and return my attention to prayer. I have found that a prayer list or journal can also help me stay focused. Wherever your location, it's important you're alone.

A Specific Purpose: He Needed to Make a Decision

Jesus spent time in prayer *before* he made major decisions. Two occasions bear this out. In the early days of ministry, Jesus was shifting locations of service.[30] If you've ever made a move, you know there's a lot involved in that decision. Jesus had previously moved his ministry operations to

Capernaum, and he was getting ready to expand his teaching circuit into the hills surrounding Galilee.[31] To do so, he would be leaving some tremendous ministry opportunities behind.[32] When Peter points this out, notice Jesus' answer: "Let us go to the next towns, that I may preach there also, for that is why I came out."[33] How did Jesus make this decision? Three verses earlier we discover the answer. Jesus was praying "early in the morning."[34] It seems reasonable that Jesus discovered his next steps through prayer.

Even more important than where he would do ministry is who would lead the ministry. The fact that Jesus didn't choose perfect people is evident in the transparency of the gospel record. Thomas doubted him. Peter denied him. Judas betrayed him. All twelve argued over who would be the greatest. Yet, prior to their selection, Jesus spent the night in prayer. Luke records, "In these days he went out to the mountain to pray, and all night he continued in prayer to God. And when day came, he called his disciples and chose from them twelve, whom he named apostles . . ."[35]

Jesus not only prayed about this selection, he literally *continued in prayer throughout the night without interruption.* When you face a major decision, do you pray like Jesus? Do you spend more time talking to God or talking to others?

There is another truth easily missed in a cursory reading. We may assume that Jesus' unique relationship with his Father spilled over into his prayer life, yet we don't see the Father *speaking back* to Jesus during his time of prayer; we just read that Jesus prayed all night long. It's not that the Father couldn't audibly speak back; on three other occasions he spoke in an audible voice so Jesus could hear.[36] Rather, the Father speaking back seems to be the exception rather than the standard.

I confess, sometimes when I've prayed over a decision

I've thought: *I just wish God would tell me what to do.* Perhaps you have, too. Not so with Jesus. He seems to have discovered his answer through the process of prayer, not because the Father gave a quick and easy answer. He labored in prayer, and so should we.

JESUS AND THE PATTERN FOR PRAYER

Jesus not only learned to pray well,[37] he taught others to pray, too. At his disciples' request, he laid out a pattern of prayer for them to follow. The Lord's Prayer may be the most repeated prayer in history.[38] I have heard it prayed at concerts and for cancer patients, at football games and funerals, as if by simple repetition one has done his spiritual duty.

The prayer is short—only 70 words. You've got to love Jesus' approach. No long lectures. No grueling homework. Fewer than 70 words and you hit the Amen button. Why would Jesus pray all night long,[39] and then teach a twenty-second prayer to the disciples? The answer: Jesus wasn't teaching a *prayer*; he was teaching a *pattern* for prayer. He assumed that they would expand their prayer time as they practiced the proper elements.

The disciples may have learned the outline, but it is apparent that they never developed their prayer life fully. When Jesus needed them to pray, they couldn't go 60 minutes without falling asleep. Pay careful attention to Jesus' question: "And he came to the disciples and found them sleeping. And he said to Peter, 'So, could you not watch with me one hour?'"[40] The disciples should have been able to stretch the twenty-second pattern into a sixty-minute prayer, but they could not. The fault didn't lie with the teacher. Although they had six months to practice the pattern, the students had not properly prepared for the test.[41] I see three components in Jesus' blueprint for prayer that we would do well to include in our own prayer time. As we give them our attention, we can grow to pray just like Jesus. They are reverence, submission, and dependence.

Reverence

Reverence is a word we don't hear much today. The casual nature of our human relationships may have left its impression on the divine. We should remember that God is not like us.[42] Jesus said "hallowed be your name." Reverencing God is to fearfully recognize that he is worthy of praise. Jesus instructs his disciples that God's name is to be set apart, pure and holy. God the Father is not like us. He is transcendent; we are not. While I appreciate that I can come to God as a friend, I want him to be a *reverenced* friend. A quick glance at creation helps me remember this truth. The Scripture says, "His eternal power and divine nature, have been clearly perceived, ever since the creation of the world, in the things that have been made."[43]

As I write this, I'm watching the sun set over the Colorado Rockies. The mountains are massive, their beauty magnificent. I look at the view and understand this verse. *His eternal power ... has been clearly perceived . . . in the things that have been made.* When I pray, I remember I am speaking to a mountain-making God. Like Job, it leaves me breathless.[44]

The Old Testament saints prayed this way too. Consider the Jewish leader Nehemiah. Living 600 miles away from his homeland, he is deeply burdened by the condition of his people back in Jerusalem. Yet, in spite of all that turmoil, Nehemiah begins his prayer with a moment of praise. Reverencing the Lord, he prays, "O LORD[45] God of heaven, the great and awesome God who keeps covenant and steadfast love with those who love him and keep his commandments."[46] Notice the focus. Nehemiah recognizes the transcendence of God (he is the God of heaven); He acknowledges the character of God (he is great and awesome); and finally, he references the work of God (he keeps his promises and steadfast love).

Just like Nehemiah, we develop a reverence for God by thinking about who he is and what he's done. I have a good friend who maintained this pattern for years. Haunted by a painful memory in her past and unable to sleep at night, she recited the qualities and names of God from A to Z. She kept a running list and later published it.[47] I usually reflect upon several of the attributes of God in my prayer time. It brings me to an attitude of reverence (See page 57 for an abridged listing of the attributes of God). Jesus instructed the disciples to begin their prayer with a time of reverence. We should do the same.

Submission

Jesus' final prayer in the garden is all about submission.[48] The placement of this prayer at the end of his earthly life is not a coincidence. Jesus learned how to submit during his daily habit of prayer, so he instructs his disciples to do the same. Six simple words: *Your kingdom come, your will be done.* Our lips speak this easily enough, but our will can be more stubborn. Praying with an attitude of submission changes us.

It is not enough to submit grudgingly and to think that we are doing something honorable. God desires our submission, even during difficult times, to be offered with a joyful attitude.[49] To submit properly is to place joyfully my will under the will of my Father's. I should desire to do his will more than mine.

Being fully human, Jesus understood the difficulty of submission of the human will. Prayer became an increasingly valuable aid to help him choose his Father's will over his personal desires. This culminates in the Garden of Gethsemane experience.[50] We tend to view his final prayer of submission as an individual event; but when you view the entirety of the gospel account, his final prayer is the culmination of practicing submission in smaller steps.[51] From Jesus we learn that our prayer life deepens as we practice submission.

Unfortunately, sometimes our prayers seem to be more about asking God to submit to our desires than us submitting to his. So what do we do when God doesn't answer our prayers in the way we desire or on the timetable of our choosing? The apostle Paul shows us how to pray in this situation. While we do not know the nature of Paul's thorn in the flesh, we do know that he asked God to remove it and God did not. Paul writes,

> A thorn was given me in the flesh, a messenger of Satan to harass me, to keep me from becoming conceited. Three times I pleaded with the Lord about this, that it should leave me. But he said to me, "My grace is sufficient for you, for my power is made perfect in weakness." Therefore I will boast all the more gladly of my weaknesses, so that the power of Christ may rest upon me. For the sake of Christ, then, I am content with weaknesses, insults, hardships, persecutions, and calamities. For when I am weak, then I am strong.[52]

Paul teaches us how to bring a request to God and still maintain a submissive spirit:

(1) We may ask God to remove our difficult circumstances.[53]
(2) We may ask more than once—both Jesus and Paul asked three times.[54]
(3) As we pray, we acknowledge that God's plan for us may be different than what we desire.[55]
(4) Finally, we submit our desires to God and trust him to give the grace necessary to do his will.[56]

No one cares to feel weak. No one likes insults. Yet the apostle Paul talked freely of his weaknesses. He expressed contentment with insults and hardships. He did not try to avoid persecutions and calamities.

Those of us who cling to comfort will struggle to pray this way. But those who desire to deepen their prayer life will consistently maintain a spirit of submission. A submissive spirit can be learned, and praying for God's grace while enduring the suffering is the place to start.

Dependence

Jesus grew in dependence on the Father for his physical and spiritual provision. He teaches the disciples to pursue the same. In our Western culture, we refrigerate more in leftovers than the poorest families in the world eat in a week. It's hard to think about praying for *daily* bread. But there it is nonetheless: a reminder from Jesus that we shouldn't go 24 hours without acknowledging that we need the Father to provide. Physical provision is only the beginning. Jesus taught the disciples that prayer is our means to depend on the Lord for *spiritual* provision. We desire forgiveness and the ability to forgive. We need protection from temptation and deliverance from evil. This is all part of depending on the Lord for our spiritual provision. All these are available through prayer.

Jesus saw prayer as an expression of dependence on the Father, as a tremendous resource in living life for God's glory. When tempted he responded, "Man shall not live by bread alone."[57] It's easy to overlook the context of Jesus' statement. He had just completed 40 days of prayer and fasting. His hunger had driven him to a greater level of dependence on the Father. He was so weakened physically that the Father sent angels to restore his strength.[58] Jesus borrowed the statement from Deuteronomy 8:3. There, Moses reminded the Israelites that their parents' hunger should have intensified their dependence on the Lord, but it only became another venue to air their complaints.[59] Jesus chose an attitude of dependence over a spirit of complaining. Prayer enabled this choice.

JESUS AND PROGRESSION IN PRAYER

Because Jesus grew in his dependence upon prayer, we would expect the most remarkable times of prayer to be at the end of his life. On that final night, Jesus expressed his total dependence on the Lord through prayer, praying for himself,[60] then for his disciples,[61] then for those of us who would later come to him.[62]

While his prayer time changed locations, his prayers did not stop. Jesus crossed over the Brook of Kidron to the Garden of Gethsemane.[63] The brook would have been flowing red with the blood from nearly 200,000 Passover lambs sacrificed at the temple over the previous two days.[64] As he moved into the garden, overwhelmed by the task before him, he depended upon a resource that was both familiar and fully developed—prayer.

Perhaps you've seen the picture of Jesus kneeling by a rock in the garden; hands folded, eyes turned upward, the perfect picture of serenity. The gospel writers paint a different picture; it doesn't include serenity. Mark records that he "fell to the ground" in distress.[65] Luke describes a dangerous condition known as *hematidrosis* in which, under extreme anguish or physical pain, the capillaries beneath the skin dilate and burst, mixing blood with perspiration.[66] Luke also records that an angel came to strengthen him.[67] Matthew tells us that Jesus pleaded three times that the "cup pass from me" – an Old Testament reference to drinking the "wrath of God." While Jesus didn't fear the crucifixion or death, he did fear—and for good reason—the judgment of his Father's righteous anger against our sin that he was about to embrace.[68]

There is nothing peaceful about this scene. The only one praying was sweating blood, physically exhausted, and emotionally drained, but still clinging to prayer in spite of heaven's silent answer. In his greatest hour of need, Jesus found prayer to be a sustaining resource, enabling him to do the will of his Father. Having prayed, he *knew* that his Father *knew* and that was enough.

Sadly, if you could have joined the prayer meeting in the garden that night, you would have heard more snoring than praying. While the disciples had been taught how to pray, they had not faithfully practiced the truths they had learned.[69] Only Jesus had grown and progressed in his prayer life to the point where he could pray with clear focus in spite of his deep distress.

In the spring of 1997, I was cleaning up our yard after a harsh winter when I heard my daughter's voice: "Daddy, mommy's crying. She needs you." I ran to the house, and as I opened the door, I could hear despair in my wife's weeping. She had just received the news that her mother had been diagnosed with a stage-four brain tumor and had less than four months to live. We packed our bags and made the 660-mile trek from New Jersey to Indiana, arriving at the hospital the next day.

While surgery had been considered, it had been put off to avoid angering the tumor. However, her rapid physical decline over the next 72 hours made surgery her only option. As a family, we gathered and prayed, attempting to prepare ourselves for what lie ahead. The doctor came from surgery with a smile of relief.   Through surgery he had discovered that it wasn't a brain tumor after all. It was a simple abscess. He had rinsed the area with antibiotics; and after a few days of recovery, she should be released to live a happy, normal life. Their earlier diagnosis had been wrong; she would be fine. Shouts rang out. Tears flowed freely. My father-in-law spontaneously hugged the doctor, thanking him again and again. We gave God thanks right there in the waiting room — it didn't matter who was watching.

We were all exhausted, but relieved. Everyone went home for the night. The sons-in-law took shifts in her room, just in case she woke up. About an hour into my shift, I noticed the nurses seemed worried. She was showing additional signs of deterioration. I asked if I should call the family. They were certain that the doctor would want to see the family first thing in the morning. So I waited, and, since I could do nothing else, I prayed. I prayed for a miracle. I prayed for my father-in-law. I prayed for my wife. I prayed for the rest of the family. I prayed for God's sustaining grace for whatever lay ahead. A hospital waiting room is a lonely place at 12:30 AM. I had a solitary place to pray, and I was awake in the early morning—just like Jesus.

Until that moment, I had always believed that if I needed to pray through the night because of a life or death need I would have no difficulty doing so, but I confess that I struggled to keep my mind focused on prayer. I fought the yawns, but they came anyway. No matter how hard I tried, I drifted in and out of sleep, just like the disciples. I had to humbly admit I was not ready to pray *like Jesus*. I could not maintain his intensity. The best I could muster was praying *like the disciples*. Five days from the date of her surgery, my mother-in-law passed into eternity. I have always regretted the fact that I was unable to pray that night like Jesus had learned to pray.

Before my feeble attempt at praying through the night, I had been incredulous at the disciple's inability to stay awake and pray in the garden. Here was the lesson, loud and clear: *Your ability to pray in your greatest need is determined by how faithfully you pray for your daily needs.*

This is why Jesus instructed the disciples to pray for their daily bread.[70] The daily practice of prayer gets you ready to pray in your greatest need. If you have not developed a pattern of praying over time, you cannot instantaneously have *that* kind of prayer life just because the situation is desperate. This was a lesson Jesus had learned well and one the disciples had not. Jesus had progressed in his prayer life to the point that when he needed to pull an all-nighter, he could.

You and I ought to be growing in our ability to pray. We may not be there yet; but as we pray consistently for daily needs, we will be ready to pray in our greatest need, just like Jesus.

THE SECOND RESOURCE:
TIME IN THE WORD

T HE LION circled, but Jesus didn't notice. He was on his knees, lost in prayer, only his lips moving. The sun beat down without mercy, the wind whipped the desert sand – there was no protection from the elements.[71] This was his 40th day without food, and the fast had stripped his body of strength. He did not look like himself. His skin stretched like shrink-wrap over a thin, skeletal frame. His once strong muscles were withered to a fraction of their size. His ribs protruded from his sides. His fingers were bony. Blisters and sores had broken out on the surface of his skin – the final expression of his malnourished state.[72]

But while his body was unrecognizable, his spirit had developed a strong sense of dependence on his Father. It was as if the strength he now lacked in his physical body had been transferred to his spirit.

The flesh and blood lion still circled, but that was the least of his worries. There was something else stalking him now; a lion of a different kind.[73]

Jesus heard the words before he saw the shape. "If you are the Son of God, command this stone to become bread." Those words elicited his strongest hunger pains yet. His stomach insisted. His body quivered for lack of strength. The memory of his mother's baking wafted up from the desert floor. The nerve endings in his fingertips sprung to life and fired the message: The stone beneath your hand feels like a loaf of bread. Just say the word.

He paused briefly before he spoke. Remembering Eve's

failure with the deceiver, he didn't want to engage a conversation; he wanted to parry with truth. His mind chased down the Biblical narratives he'd learned as a child. He was looking for parallels to his situation.

The wilderness. The desires of his people. The nagging hunger pains. He had the story. He could see the letters on the scroll. His mind raced to the final verse. He opened his mouth and spoke. "It is written, 'Man shall not live by bread alone.'"[74]

The written Word had authority. It emptied the deception of its power. In a moment the mirage of his mother's oven was gone. His hunger subsided. And his fingertips told him the truth: *The stone beneath your hand feels like … a stone.*

The deceiver couldn't argue. Still, he continued to circle. Perhaps he could change the subject.

J ESUS knew the Word well. He could pull out an obscure Bible passage, explain its meaning, and the people would stand amazed.[75] When tempted by Satan, he answered with Scriptures that he had carefully considered and properly applied.[76] When others had a need, Jesus listened well and had the right passage to share.[77]

Because he operated within the intrinsic limitations of humanity, he acquired his skill with the Word through learning. The Bible declares that he *grew* in wisdom and favor with God.[78] Like all young Jewish boys, he would have memorized a significant portion of the Scripture. To gain such knowledge, Jesus studied, learned, memorized, and applied. Do we bring the same kind of diligent study to the Word that Jesus brought?

Imagine that your physical health was failing. Your energy level was way down, and you were susceptible to nearly every sickness. You visit the family doctor, and he begins his exam with some questions. "Are you sleeping well?" "Yes," you reply, "I'm sleeping nearly all the time." The doctor ponders your answer and asks the next question. "How is your appetite? Are you eating regularly?" "Oh yes, doctor, I'm eating one good meal a week; occasionally I'll grab a snack Monday through Friday if my schedule allows it."

The doctor looks up from his notepad. "I believe I misunderstood you. I thought you said you were eating one good meal a week. No one can survive on that diet! No wonder you're susceptible to so many diseases. It's easy to see why you have no energy. Your body needs more food than one good meal a week. I'm recommending three good meals a day." You look up from the examination table, troubled, "But doctor, I don't have time to eat that often, and besides, it's so hard. That means I'd have to prepare some of my own meals."

Most Christians would never do to their physical bodies what they do to their spirits. If your entire spiritual diet consists of one service on Sunday, you are sure to be malnourished. If you hope to feed your soul regularly from the Word, you will have to prepare your own meals. Bible study, application, and memorization are everyday necessities as you grow in Christ.[79] Paul wrote to Timothy, "Study to show yourself approved unto God, a workman who needs not to be ashamed."[80]

I have chosen to emphasize three areas of personal

study that are essential for your spiritual growth: (1) study-ing the Word for discovery; (2) applying the Word for change; (3) memorizing the Word for instant retrieval.

STEP 1: STUDYING THE WORD FOR DISCOVERY

Consider this: the Bible was written thousands of years ago to a culture with which we are unfamiliar and in a language most of us have never learned. Over time the meanings of words change, and cultures shift; therefore, careful, diligent study of the Word will be necessary for understanding its intended meaning. Five steps will prove helpful.

(1) Pray Humbly

In Psalm 119:18 we read, "Open my eyes, that I may behold wondrous things out of your law." When we pray, we are acknowledging we need God's help to understand his Word. The verses surrounding the Psalmist's prayer give direction for how we ought to pray prior to time in the Word. Verse 19 says, "hide not your commandments from me." In other words, we desire to know the meaning of the given text. Properly understanding the text is essential. Verse 17 says "that I might know and keep your word." Prayer is preparation to not only *know* but also *do* what God reveals from our study. This humble posture is essential for meaningful Bible study. What better way to discover the author's intent than to ask him for guidance when you open the Word?

(2) Read Consistently

One important step in reading the Bible is to do it daily. While not a large book (most Bibles are less than

1,000 pages), reading daily allows for reflection on a particular passage each day. There are numerous ways to read through the Bible. Consider one of the following:

- *Read through one book of the Bible for 30 days.* While there are 66 books in the Bible, investing your effort in one book for an entire month will give you a much greater understanding of that book.

- *Read a key chapter of the Bible each day.* This approach allows you to get an overview of the key characters and events in the biblical story. If you've never developed the habit of spending time in the Word daily, this is a great way to start (see page 58 for 365 key chapters).

- *Read the Bible through chronologically.* The Bible was recorded using different styles of writing (history, poetry, prophecy, and letters to individuals or groups of people). The grouping of the books in the Bible is by the writing genre instead of the order of events. For the reader unaware of this fact, the Bible can seem confusing. Visit www.biblicalstrategies.com for a chronological reading schedule and additional study resources.

(3) Observe Carefully

As you read, pay attention to the details. If you've read a passage before, don't assume you can no longer glean anything from it. Some of my greatest discoveries have come from rereading a passage. If you remain attentive, the more you read, the more you see. Here are a few tips.

- *Mark up your Bible.* As you read, keep a highlighter handy. Underline or circle key words, phrases, or verses.

- *Be attentive while you're reading.* Bible professor Dr. Howard Hendricks says to look for: (1) things that are emphasized; (2) things that are repeated; (3) things that are related; (4) things that are alike; (5) things that are unalike; (6) things that are true to life.[81]

- *Journal your discoveries.* Write down what you're learning. These are questions I've used in the past to get my journaling started. Eventually these questions will become instinctive in your observation process. What is the most obvious Bible truth I've learned? What have I learned about the character of God? Are there words or ideas that are repeated in the passage? If so, what are they? Are there words that I don't understand? What do they mean? Are there other passages in the Bible that help me understand this verse?

(4) Interpret Contextually.

Most of us hate being misinterpreted. If you have ever attempted to clear up a misunderstanding, you've probably said, "That is what I said, but it's not what I meant." Meaning matters in communication. To misinterpret someone's words, you need only take them out of context. For instance, if I say, "He's on fire!" I could be referring to a five-year old with a fever, a man running from a burning building, or an American Idol contestant advancing to the finals. The context gives the meaning.

Imagine a target with your verse as the bulls-eye. In archery, the circles closer to the bulls-eye carry greater point value; likewise, the verses closer to your verse carry greater interpretive weight.

- What do the verses before or after your verse say?
- What does the author say elsewhere about this idea?
- What does the rest of the Bible say?

My great grandmother grew up in rural Indiana. Although

she never went to high school, she developed a keen sense of discernment. Grams heard her share of preachers in her life – both good and bad. After hearing some, she would shake her head and say, "The poor Lord; he gets blamed for so many things." She understood the surest way to misinterpret God's Word was to simply take the verses out of their context.

(5) Study Diligently

For many of us, reading and studying do not come easily. Yet, when we develop these habits around our time in the Word, it bears long-lasting rewards. Pastor Zach Schlegel reminds us to have the right heart, time, place, and plan.

- *The prepared heart.* Your heart should be expectant, willing to obey, teachable, and humble. Before you open the Word, pause and prepare your heart. Humility is essential.

- *The right time.* The right time will be the time that works best for you. When are you the most alert, focused, and fresh? I had a seminary professor who did his best studying at 3:30 AM. A friend of mind commented, "Phil, God's not even up at that hour!" Your best time might be early in the morning or late at night. Pick the time that's best for you and stick with it.

- *The best place.* The best place will be one free from distractions. Pretend you just boarded the plane and "turn off all electronic devices!"

- *The committed plan.* Whether or not you are a planner, you will still need to discipline yourself to study the

Scriptures diligently. Elton Trueblood reminds us,

> We have not advanced very far in our spiritual lives if we have not encountered the basic paradox of freedom . . . that we are most free when we are bound. But not just any way of being bound will suffice; what matters is the character of our binding. The one who would be an athlete, but who is unwilling to discipline his body by regular exercise and abstinence . . . is not free to excel on the field or the track. His failure to train rigorously denies him the freedom to run with the desired speed and endurance. With one concerted voice, the giants of the devotional life apply the same principle to the whole of life: Discipline is the price of freedom.[82]

STEP 2: APPLYING THE WORD FOR CHANGE

Jesus was a doer of the Word, not just a hearer. When we walk like Jesus, the same can be said of us. The ancient Greeks saw learning as the acquisition of knowledge, but the Hebrew mindset held that true knowledge was revealed when we could practice the truth. To grow and change, you will need to apply the biblical truth you are discovering. Consider these biblical teachings:

- But be doers of the word, and not hearers only, deceiving yourselves.[83]

- So whoever knows the right thing to do and fails to do it, for him it is sin.[84]

- Teach these new disciples to obey all the commands I have given you.[85]

In his insightful book *Expository Listening*, Pastor Ken Ramey stresses the importance of the application process. While he is addressing the listener's role in hearing a message, the same could be said of our personal time in the Word:

> A proper response to God's Word begins by having an open, receptive heart. But it is not enough to just humbly and gladly accept the Word. You must act on it. You must be reactive to the Word. A chemical reaction is when chemicals undergo change. Perhaps you remember those high school chemistry experiments, when the test tube boils over after mixing two chemicals together. When you hear and receive God's Word, it should immediately elicit some kind of reaction. It should produce some change in you.[86]

Ramey further points out that there is a direct connection between listening and obeying in our Bibles. He concludes,

> The Old Testament word for "hear" is *sama*. This is the same Hebrew word used for "obey" . . . the implication is that, in God's mind, hearing and obeying are one in the same.[87]

As you read and study the Word, ask yourself the following questions: *Where does my thinking need to change? Is my attitude in need of correction? How about my actions? Are my words what they should be?*

Your time in the Word is incomplete unless you apply the truth. Jesus berated the religious leaders of his day because they taught truth but had not yet applied it personally. Note his words:

> The scribes and the Pharisees sit on Moses' seat, so practice and observe whatever they tell you—but not what they do. For they preach, but do not practice.[88]

The Old Testament scribe Ezra understood the connection between his *study* and *application*. One short verse summarized his life: "For Ezra had set his heart *to study* the Law of the LORD, and *to do* it and *to teach* his statutes and rules in Israel."[89]

When Ezra studied the Word, he first applied it to himself before he attempted to teach it to another. Like Jesus, such personal application gave Ezra's teaching authority and his life integrity. Only when he had *studied*, then *lived* it, did he *teach* it.

A number of years ago, I was vacationing with one of my uncles. After filling the car with gas, we walked into the filling station to pay the attendant. A young man stood at the counter; behind him, a copy of the Ten Commandments had been posted on the wall.

My uncle has never been slow to start a conversation, so he spoke first. "Who hung *those* up?"

"The Ten Commandments?" the young man thumbed over his shoulder. "My boss put 'em there."

"Your boss" my uncle said, "Is he a talker or a doer?"

The young man didn't hesitate, "Sir, my boss is a doer, he ain't just no talker."

"Glad to hear it," my uncle said, as we turned and left the garage.

The conversation was short, but those seven words have hung around in my memory for 20 years. *Is he a talker or a doer?* If that question was asked about me, how would those closest to me respond? And what if it was asked of those who know you best? Could it be said, "He's a doer, he ain't just no talker."

STEP 3: MEMORIZE THE WORD FOR RETRIEVAL

I first met Alexei Brenza when I taught at the seminary he founded. The man understood suffering first hand. The Ukrainian pastor had lived his life under constant harassment from Soviet Union officials. His children were taken from his care and placed in de-brainwashing classes by the Soviet leadership in an attempt to thwart their father's biblical teaching. His fellow pastors lost their lives. Threats of imprisonment and torture were constant. Still, he served with faithfulness for decades. And during these times of suffering, he found the Scriptures to be a tremendous resource.

The fall of the Soviet Union in the early 1990s opened up the door for ministry without harassment, and Brenza got busy. He founded the Irpin Theological Seminary which has graduated more than 1,000 pastors since its inception.

In spite of his notable success over the next two decades, Brenza never lost his confidence in the Scriptures as a resource during times of suffering. He was a diabetic and underwent numerous surgeries and several amputations before his death in 2010. Following one of those surgeries, and prior to the anesthesia fully wearing off, his nurse noticed his lips were moving. Assuming he was in need, she came to his bedside and placed her ear next to his lips. To her surprise, she discovered he was quoting extended portions of the Old Testament book of Hosea, even though he was not fully coherent!

Can you imagine? Most Christians I know haven't even read the book of Hosea, let alone memorized it. But suffering and the Scriptures have more in common than their first letter. Brezna knew both first hand.

It's not that we can't memorize like Brezna, it's that we choose not to do so. Paul Reber, professor of psychology at Northwestern University, describes the brain's remarkable ability to retain information:

The human brain consists of about one billion neurons . . . the brain's memory storage capacity . . . is around 2.5 petabytes (or a million gigabytes). For comparison, if your brain worked like a digital video recorder in a television, 2.5 petabytes would be enough to hold three million hours of TV shows. You would have to leave the TV running continuously for more than 300 years to use up all that storage.[90]

So if Scripture memory is important for our spiritual growth, and if our ability to remember is nearly limitless, why have not more Christians given themselves to this practice? Perhaps at least one consideration is their pride. We don't memorize because we don't think we *need* to memorize. Yet God warned us that pride would lead to our sure and certain fall.[91] When it comes to battling temptation, the humility principle works like this: Only the humble of heart will see the need to memorize the Scripture. Jesus modeled humility. The Bible says, "And being found in human form, he humbled himself."[92]

Jesus' immediate response to the tempter was to answer with God's Word.[93] Here's a question: if the Son of God deemed it necessary to memorize the Scripture to defend himself against temptation, why would we think we're exempt? Satan's clearest line of attack in temptation is directed at the pride of man. It was with Adam and Eve,[94] and it was with Jesus.[95]

To attempt a rational conversation with the tempter in the midst of temptation is a dangerous proposal. Even the powerful archangel, Michael, didn't attempt a conversation with Satan. Notice Jude's words, "But when the archangel Michael, contending with the devil, was disputing about the body of Moses, he did not presume to pronounce a blasphemous judgment, but said, "*The Lord rebuke you*" [emphasis added].[96]

To answer temptation with the Scripture is to let the Lord rebuke the tempter. We often naively attempt to do what neither the Son of God nor the archangel dared: to reason our way through temptation in our own power. How much better to simply respond with the appropriate Scripture? There is no better way to gain instant access to the Biblical passage then through memorizing it—just like Jesus.

Memorize Phrase by Phrase

The Scripture provides the method for memorizing its rich truth. Isaiah recorded, "To whom will he teach knowledge . . . For it is precept upon precept . . . line upon line . . . here a little, there a little."[97] The best way I have found to retain biblical passages is to learn a phrase, repeat it until I've mastered it, then move on to the next phrase. Once I have the phrases mastered, I begin to link them together. Sometimes I will alter my emphasis on certain words in the phrase; other times I will alter the location where I'm memorizing (my office, the car, my home), but always I am working the phrases and adding the subsequent phrase. As the Scripture says, *line upon line, here a little, there a little.*

Memorize Day by Day

When it comes to memorizing, I have found it to be more effective to spend a few minutes several times a day, as opposed to a lot of time one day during the week. Simply put, for your mind to permanently retain a truth, you will need to learn it more than once. For me the pattern works like this: Learn it once. Forget it. Relearn it. Forget it again. Relearn it again. Forget less. Relearn it again. Retain it.

While it may sound odd, forgetting is actually a significant part of memory retention. Remembering my need to forget keeps me from growing discouraged. Scripture memory is more of a process than a single event. Having worked on a verse for several days doesn't mean I will remember it tomorrow morning. I now see the process of forgetting as an essential part of learning the verse.

Memorize Sin by Sin

When Jesus was tempted in the wilderness, he responded with Scripture.[98] The Word flowed from his mind to his lips and emptied the deception of its power. Satan was powerless and departed until an opportune time.[99] To know your opponent's *modus operandi* is essential in any field. When Jesus was tempted, he responded with the Scripture because he understood Satan's techniques. Imagine what would be possible if you studied your personal struggle with temptation the way a professional athlete studied his opponent. Sportswriter Pete Prisco explains it best:

> Watching film, or tape to be precise, is key to the success of any quarterback no matter the level of play. But in the NFL, it's even more so with all the complicated defenses and looks now thrown at quarterbacks, who must decipher it all in split-second decisions or risk throwing an interception that will show up on all the highlight shows. They'd better know their stuff, and know it well . . . quarterback Peyton Manning is legendary in his film study. He has a film room in his basement. Manning loves studying tape, almost needs it like a drug. Others don't put in the time and end up in quarterback bust-land.[100]

When you read the temptation account of Jesus, it's easy to see that he understood his opponent. As Satan tempts through deception, Jesus answers with God's Word of truth. His remarkable ability to recall the right Scripture for the specific situation is the pattern we should emulate.

If you could watch a tape of your opponent, you would see that deception is his regular method of temptation. He returns to it again and again. But what Satan lacks in originality, he makes up for in thoroughness. He is mercilessly meticulous. He understands the desires of the human heart and the best way to lure and entice us to sin.[101]

However, because Satan often returns to deception as his means of temptation, you and I can plan for his attack. Jesus did. He knew the right verse for each situation. A part of my game plan has been to memorize the Scripture in conjunction with Satan's lies.

Satan, as the deceiver, often brings his temptations in the same way.[102] Some time ago, it occurred to me that if I could memorize the *lie* that Satan brought, and the corresponding *truth* from God's Word, I would be more prepared for the temptations I faced. This was the kind of reliance Jesus had upon the Scripture.[103] He had the right verse for each specific situation.

While it may seem a little intimidating at the start, anyone who memorizes the Scripture will reap tremendous dividends in his spiritual life. Just take it phrase by phrase, day by day, and sin by sin.

THE THIRD RESOURCE: DEPENDENCE ON THE SPIRIT

J ESUS stepped out of his sandals and into the muddy Jordan. For the first time he noticed the weariness of his feet as the river drifted lazily over them. He had traveled south for three days to get to where the baptizer was working.[104]

"I am the voice of one crying out in the wilderness. Make straight the way of the Lord!"[105] John's voice stirred the crowd that had gathered. Jesus stepped forward into the deeper water drawing ever closer to the one who was baptizing. There was a hint of wonder in John's tone as he asked Jesus the question, "I need to be baptized by you, and do you come to me?" Jesus smiled and answered, "This is the proper way to do everything God requires of us."[106]

Descending into the water, Jesus felt the urge to pray.[107] His lips were moving in a prayer even as he was going under. As he came up from the muddy water, he lifted his face to heaven and kept praying. Earlier he had discovered some of what his Father was asking him do, and now he was affirming his willingness . . . and waiting.

The clouds parted. The sun shone brightly. Or was it more than the sun? For those standing on the shore it appeared as if heaven's light was shining only on a man in the middle of the river. His face and hands were uplifted in prayer . . . still waiting.

John stepped back, his eyes drawn heavenward in wonder. He had baptized hundreds before, but the likes of this he had never seen. The light was descending. Slowly. Holding . . . Holding . . . Holding. Floating like a dove over the waiting man. Then suddenly the light was gone — almost as if it had entered the man standing waist deep in the river.[108]

It was only then that they heard his voice, the source indistinguishable, but not the words. "This is my Son, my beloved, in whom I am well pleased."[109] Still standing in the river, Jesus lowered his hands. He looked around at the people's faces and smiled. They were the reason he had come. He began to move towards the shore. As he did, he felt within him a power he had not previously known. It was through this power that he could help them in their greatest need.

For those who were watching from the shoreline, it appeared as though he left the river differently than he went in. He had gone in of his own accord, but as he neared the shore, it was as if someone was leading him.[110] Like a guide, but invisible to the eyes of the watchers. . .

W HEN IT comes to depending on resources, I usually prefer those that I can see. Yet the Holy Spirit is invisible to my human eyes. This is why I am so thankful for Jesus. Operating under the intrinsic limitation of humanity, Jesus shows us how to interact with the Holy Spirit. He leaned on the Spirit of God as a resource who, in turn, *filled* and *led* him to do the work of his Father.[111]

JESUS WAS FULL OF THE HOLY SPIRIT

Among the gospel writers, only Luke recorded that Jesus was full of the Holy Spirit. He writes, "And Jesus, full of the Holy Spirit, returned from the Jordan and was led by the Spirit in the wilderness."[112]

The word he chose was one that connotes "abundance, completion, and perfection."[113] Our tendency may be to think of this as a unique relationship that the Holy Spirit has with Jesus because of their eternal relationship within the Godhead. Yet, Luke uses the same terminology in the book of Acts to describe the church's first martyr, Steven, when he writes, "But he [Stephen], full of the Holy Spirit, gazed into heaven and saw the glory of God, and Jesus standing at the right hand of God."[114]

To be full of the Holy Spirit is to be under his control.[115] This "filling" was not only true of Jesus and Steven; it should be true of all who are believers. Paul gives an even clearer understanding of the Spirit controlled life in his letter to the Ephesians. He writes, "And do not get drunk with wine, for that is debauchery, but be filled with the Spirit.[116]

When someone has had too much to drink, we say that they are no longer "in control." By becoming intoxicated, they have chosen to relinquish their control to another substance. This is the meaning behind the word *filled*. Paul warns us not to be "under the control" of alcohol, but rather to be "under the control of the Holy Spirit."

He carefully chose the verb "be filled" to reveal four essential elements about our relationship with the Holy Spirit. Each of these is hidden in the Greek grammar. Among other things, the Greek language communicates the meaning of its verbs through mood, form, voice, and tense. When it comes to being filled with the Spirit, consider:

(1) This isn't Optional.

"Be filled" is in the imperative mood. The imperative

mood is one of command. When our mom gave a command, we knew it wasn't optional. God wanted us to know that being filled with the Spirit is not optional, so he chose the mood of command.

(2) This is for All of Us.

"Be filled" is in the plural form. Being filled with the Spirit is not simply for a few – the spiritually elite or hyper-religious – it is a command given for each of us. No one is excluded from this command, so God chose the "all-inclusive" plural form.

(3) This Happens to Us, Not by Us.

"Be filled" is in the passive voice. The active voice is the doer of the action, but the passive voice is the receiver of the action. Imagine I am holding a pitcher filled with water and you are holding an empty glass. If you wish for your glass to be filled, as I begin pouring the water from the pitcher, you don't fill your glass; you simply move your glass so that I can fill it. This isn't simply true of pitchers and glasses. It is true of our relationship with the Spirit; he does the filling, we do the obeying. When we are submitting to his will through our obedience to the Word, we are doing our part. We can trust the Spirit to do his.

(4) This is a Repeated Event.

"Be filled" is in the present tense. Some have properly translated it "be being filled." The present tense implies a daily, moment-by-moment, repeated event. I remember an old preacher who once said he needed to be filled with the Holy Spirit every day because he leaked! That's a good reminder for all of us.

Because Jesus was fully human, he chose not to follow his feelings, but to be controlled by the Spirit. This idea is clearly apparent in the temptation.[117] While we can be certain Jesus was very hungry, having gone 40 days without eating, he chose not to surrender to his feelings but to submit to the Spirit's control. Jesus saw surrendering to the Spirit's control as an essential resource to living a God-honoring life. He did this daily, and he did it willingly.

JESUS WAS LED BY THE SPIRIT

Jesus allowed himself to be led by the Spirit. Anyone following Christ will do the same. Luke records, "And Jesus, full of the Holy Spirit, returned from the Jordan and was led by the Spirit in the wilderness."[118] In the 5th chapter of Galatians, Paul gives four commands that capture this same idea. Each is uniquely associated with walking. He says we are to: be led by the Spirit; walk in the Spirit; live by the Spirit; and keep in step with the Spirit.[119] This is instructive; *walking* is the biblical metaphor to describe daily habits. John MacArthur explains,

> The fact that *peripateō* (walk) is used here in the present tense indicates that Paul is speaking of continuous, regular action, in other words, a habitual way of life. And the fact that the verb is also in the imperative mood indicates he is not giving believers an option but a command. Among other things, walking implies progress, going from where one is to where he ought to be. As a believer submits to the Spirit's control, he moves forward in his spiritual life. Step by step the Spirit moves him from where he is toward where God wants him to be.[120]

By tracing the word "walk" through Paul's letters, we discover four truths about these daily habits God wants us to develop as we depend upon the Spirit.

(1) Be Attentive: Developing Daily Habits is Dangerous.

Good habits are hard to maintain, and bad habits are hard to break. Things done daily can be dangerous because they so easily become habits. The Scripture warns, "Look carefully then how you walk, not as unwise but as wise, making the best use of the time, because the days are evil."[121] We typically don't think of walking as dangerous; but when we start to take those first steps, we have no idea where they will take us.

On October 20, 1970, Dave and John Kunst started walking east out of their hometown of Waseca, Minnesota. Twenty pairs of shoes and 14,450 miles later, Dave Kuntz walked back into his home town from the west side, having become the first person to circle the land mass of the earth by walking. His brother never returned, having been shot and killed by bandits in Afghanistan two years into their journey. When the Kunst brothers left town that October they never considered that only one would return.

Walking can be dangerous. So are daily habits. Ask the forty year old man who was introduced to pornography when he was thirteen, or the woman facing retirement who desperately wants to be victorious in her life-long battle with alcohol. Consider the person who gossips so frequently they are not even aware they are doing it, or the man who feels trapped in his bitterness and resentment. The Scriptures warn us to develop daily habits *carefully*. Don't let more than 24 hours go by without considering whether your choices are wise or unwise.

(2) Be Patient: Developing Daily Habits Requires Small Steps.

The Scripture offers this reminder:

> Do not be deceived: God is not mocked, for whatever one sows, that will he also reap. For the one who sows to his own flesh will from the flesh reap corruption, but the one who sows to the Spirit will from the Spirit reap eternal life.[122]

The sowing and reaping metaphor is found within eight verses of God's reminder to "walk in the Spirit." Because of our tendency toward impatience, this word picture has a note of encouragement attached: "Let us not grow weary of doing good, for in due season we will reap, if we do not give up."[123] The practice of "sowing and reaping" reminds us that patience is a requirement when daily habits are being developed. The new habits may spring up overnight, but they won't bear fruit overnight.

An equation I've often shared is: success = short-term goals + high accountability. Becoming like Christ won't happen instantly. New habits take time to bear fruit. Until the new habits are a part of your daily routine, you will find accountability helpful. Do the task daily; it will become a habit. Do the habit consistently; it will bear fruit.

My dad was a farmer. Farming always remained a part of his life, even after he went to college to become a school teacher. He loved to see things grow. One of my earliest recollections with my dad was us kneeling down in the soil of our Indiana farm with our faces close to the ground. There we could see the corn just popping through the surface. Never did my dad brag about how he made the corn grow. He saw himself responsible for the sowing, weeding, feeding, protecting, and harvesting of the crop, but not the growing. Here's the lesson every farmer knows: you do the sowing, God does the growing.

The same is true of our growth in Christ. One of the reasons we grow discouraged with slow growth is because we believe that we are in some way responsible for the growth. Remember: *you do the sowing, God does the growing*. Learn to stay busy with the daily tasks, and God will make your life fruitful. Be patient. Developing daily habits requires small steps. Rejoice in the growth you do see, and pray to the Lord of the harvest that more growth may appear.

(3) Be Focused: Developing Daily Habits Requires Changing Thought Patterns.

We often think of habits as the things that we do. Yet, few things become habits so quickly as the thoughts that we think. You probably do a number of "mindless" tasks to prepare to go to work or school in the morning. But, are they really "mindless?" Or are they mental habits? Things like: brushing your teeth, taking a shower, pouring the cereal, and making the coffee. Our hurried culture even captures this truth. We say: "I never gave it a second thought." Are we not implying that we gave it a first thought?

This truth brings both good news and bad. The good news is that our thoughts are only habits, not involuntary actions. So, by the power of the Spirit, we can choose what we think about. There is hope for the destruction of old thought patterns and the development of new ones. The bad news is that, because these thoughts come so quickly and frequently, they are challenging to break. This is why the Scripture says,

> . . . You formerly walked according to the course of
> this world, according to the prince of the power of the
> air, of the spirit that is now working in the sons of
> disobedience. Among them we too all formerly lived in
> the lusts of our flesh, indulging the desires of the flesh
> and of the mind. . .[124]

The biblical passage is an excellent reminder of the
location of our battlefield. When we formerly lived in the
lusts of the flesh, we indulged our desires and our minds.
Walking in the Spirit means we develop a new set of
thought patterns that help us control those sinful desires.
There are different Greek words that the translators of
Scripture captured with the word "mind." The one used
here could also be translated as *understanding* or *imagination*.[125]

What are you imagining right now? What are you
thinking? Are your imaginative fantasies developed from
the "course of this world" or from the "mind of your Master?" Are you bending your mind around a sexual fantasy?
Are you dreaming about how you might spend a million
dollars? Are you imagining the pleasure of the upcoming
weekend or retirement? Such imaginations are thinking
like the world. Your thoughts are all about you. There is
nothing of the sweet service of Jesus[126] in them. This is why
Paul challenged us to control our minds.[127] He also gave this
strict warning ". . . do not be conformed to this world, but
be transformed by the renewing of your mind."[128]

One of my favorite childhood memories was hearing
my grandfather say grace at the table. I confess it wasn't my
favorite memory at the time, because his prayers were long
and grandma's cooking was good! But you always knew

when Grandpa's prayer was coming to an end, because he would say, "Lord, forgive us where we have sinned against you in word, deed, or thought." In his simple way he grasped the importance of one's thinking in order for him to be victorious over sin. My Grandpa understood that if you were headed into battle you better know the location of the battlefield.

(4) Be Encouraged: Developing Daily Habits Implies Progress.

Because developing new habits is difficult and we are prone to grow discouraged, the Scripture gives this reminder: "We are his workmanship, created in Christ Jesus for good works, which God prepared beforehand, that we should walk in them."[129]

The question "Where will you go when you die?" has certainly caused many to think about their eternal destiny. Yet, if we only think about salvation as an eternal matter, we will miss much of what God expects of us this side of heaven and we will grow easily discouraged. Here is the reason: as a new creation in Christ, your purpose for living has changed. You may not have thought about it that way at the time. You may have just seen yourself as a lost sinner in need of a Savior. But Ephesians 2:10 reminds us that "we were created in Christ Jesus for good works." God didn't save us to alter only our *eternal* destiny; he recreated us to bring him glory *now*.

Prior to salvation, we were driven by our pleasures and attempted to satisfy them.[130] While those old desires are still hanging around, our new purpose is to accomplish the good works that God has prepared for us to do.[131] We are *his* workmanship, not our own. We live for *him*, not ourselves.

This is where the image of the crucifixion is helpful to encourage the believer's new change of purpose. We tend to limit the crucifixion to what happened to *Jesus* at a point in history, but Paul saw the crucifixion as what happened to *him* when Jesus was crucified. He encourages us to do the same. Notice what he says: "I have been crucified with Christ. It is no longer I who live, but Christ who lives in me. And the life I now live in the flesh I live by faith in the Son of God, who loved me and gave himself for me."[132]

Motivated by the love Jesus had for him, Paul now lives his life loving others. Just like Jesus gave himself for Paul, Paul desires to give himself for others – and in so doing, he brings glory to God. He no longer does works for himself, but for his Master.[133] This is why his works are considered good.

Prior to the fall of man, God looked upon his creation and saw that it was simply *good*,[134] but on the sixth day of creation (after creating man) God saw that it was *very* good. Why the distinction? Because man alone was made in the image of God. He could bring God glory like nothing else in creation. When man fell, he lost more than his relationship with God; he lost his divine purpose for living. When we become a new creation in Christ, we are enabled to fulfill that divine purpose again. Nothing in this life brings encouragement like doing what you were created to do. Remember, *walking* is the New Testament metaphor for daily habits. So we are told to "walk in good works." Develop the daily habit of doing what you were called to do.

For years our family has spent a week of every summer with my wife's family in the Colorado Rockies. *Lost Valley Ranch* is located in the Pike's Peak National forest. The floor of the valley is surrounded by climbable mountains, and every summer I enjoy taking hikes in those mountains. *Enjoy* is a relative term. For someone who is used to breathing oxygen at sea level 51 weeks out of the year, it is hard work walking more than 100 paces when you're a mile and a half high. What I really enjoy is looking back when I get to my destination.

Walking in good works is a lot like hiking in the mountains. It's hard work, but just like God empowers my physical body to walk at high altitudes, he empowers my spirit to do works for him I never dreamed possible. We find encouragement for the daily task because we are doing what we were *recreated* to do all along. This is the final step of walking in the Spirit. Be encouraged. Only God could make such a thing possible.

SURRENDERING TO THE ONE I CAN'T SEE

My friend Mike is training to run a marathon. He's in his fifties, so he watches what he eats and gets up early to run several days a week with friends. He's always loved running. He once told me that he feels total freedom when he runs, but you'll never see Mike run alone. He always runs with friends. He's up to a half marathon now – running with a friend on his left and a friend on his right. It's not that he lacks the courage to run alone; on the contrary, he has exceptional courage. Mike is legally blind. When he runs, he holds on to one end of a shoe string and his friend holds the other end. So while he cannot see where he's running, he can still know the freedom he knew prior to losing his eyesight in his twenties.

Running for Mike is only possible because he is willing to be led. His willingness to follow another communicates a tremendous amount of trust in his running partners. He needs them. He depends on them even if they lead him down a path he may not have chosen for himself. He pays a great deal of attention to the slightest movement of the shoe string.

It is said of Jesus that he was led by the Spirit into the wilderness.[135] Jesus was willing to follow, even when it meant going to a place that he might not have chosen for himself. This seems to be the strength behind Mark's choice of words when he writes, "The Spirit immediately drove him out into the wilderness. And he was in the wilderness forty days, being tempted by Satan. And he was with the wild animals, and the angels were ministering to him."[136]

It's not that Jesus was reluctant. On the contrary, he was full of the Spirit and led by the Spirit.[137] However, he may not have chosen to travel so deeply into the wilderness at this stage of his ministry; he trusted the Spirit. Such is the nature of being led.

Paul uses the phrase "led by the Spirit" to describe our daily dependence on God.

- "For all who are *led by the Spirit of God* are sons of God."[138]
- "For the desires of the flesh are against the Spirit, and the desires of the Spirit are against the flesh, for these are opposed to each other, to keep you from doing the things you want to do. But if you are *led by the Spirit*, you are not under the law."[139]

It is significant that both times Paul uses the phrase "led by the Spirit" it is in the context of one's battle with temptation. This is the context for Jesus as well.[140] Clearly the lesson is this: our greatest need for dependence on the Holy

Spirit takes place during our greatest times of temptation.

How might that change the nature of your battle with temptation? What if, when the desires of your heart began to heat up, you gave your undivided attention to the leading of the Holy Spirit? Like Mike, my marathon-running friend, your mind would be focused on the slightest movement of the shoestrings.

The Holy Spirit didn't lead Jesus into temptation; he led Jesus through the temptation.[141] Jesus needed to be willing to let him lead. So do you, and so do I.

Conclusion:
Committing to Live Just Like Jesus

My daughter and I ascended the steps of The Philadelphia Museum of Art on a Sunday afternoon. The falling rain was not a deterrent for those giving their best Sylvester Stallone impressions for their friends' cameras. But we had not come to see Rocky Balboa look-alikes; we had come to see what Rembrandt thought Jesus *looked* like.

The Faces of Jesus was a traveling exhibition that brought together Rembrandt's paintings of Jesus. The galleries told the story of how previous artists had attempted to deify their pictures of Jesus – intentionally making him look *unlike* us. Examples of this type of art were hanging in the first rooms we walked through. Then we came to galleries containing Rembrandt's work. While it was crowded, there was a hush in the room. You could almost read the thoughts of believer and unbeliever alike: *was this what Jesus looked like*?

While not an artist, I, too, studied the pictures. I was intrigued by how much Jesus had in common with us. If Rembrandt's Jesus walked into the room, you would be unable to pick him out of the crowd. He looked so very human. That's when it struck me: the portraits of Jesus looked human because he was human. While being fully God, Jesus lived out his entire human life under the intrinsic limitations of humanity. He lived this earthly life leaning heavily on three resources: prayer, the Word, and the Spirit. Today he invites you to do the same. Stop using the Jesus-was-God excuse, and start walking just like Jesus. Remember the truth behind the incarnation of Christ: He walked where you walk so that you might learn to walk just like he walked.

You might need to reconsider how you have been thinking about Jesus. Rembrandt did. One man's imagination reshaped the way generations not yet born would see the face of their Savior.

God is calling you to do the same. Reshape the image of Jesus in the minds of those who are watching you. Show them a Jesus who is three-dimensional: active, living and growing. Jesus grew. So can you. Start growing today. Just like Jesus.

And the Word became flesh and dwelt among us, and we
have seen his glory, glory as of the only Son from the
Father, full of grace and truth.
John 1:14

Whoever says he abides in him ought to walk
in the same way in which he walked.
1 John 2:6

Creating a Prayer Journal

- Taking an 8.5 by 11 sheet of paper, fold it in half three times. When you unfold the paper, you will find creases that comprise 8 identical compartments. Title the first "every day"; then starting with "Sunday", title the remaining 7 compartments for each day of the week. Place your every day requests in the first box, and divide the rest of your requests among the days of the week. Folding it up, you have a pocket sized journal to get started.

- *The Pocket Prayer Journal* is an APP for your I-phone that allows you to record the request, mark them as answered, not answered, overdue, etc.

The 10 Minute Prayer Pattern: PRAY

The *PRAY* acrostic is a memory device for prayer. It can be as short as a few minutes, or you may include more time as God leads. PRAY stands for Praise, Repent, Ask, and Yield.

(1) Praise – At the beginning of prayer, praise the *who*, *what*, and *why* of God. Praise him for *who* he is by reflecting upon his character. When you remember *what* he's done, you are meditating on his works. Finally, remember the *why* of God. Often he is motivated by his steadfast love towards us (Psalm 100:5).

(2) Repent – Once you've thought about what God has done, you can move easily to what you haven't done. Repentance takes place when we remember our failures and turn from them. A humble confession in prayer reveals a dependence on the Spirit in order to be restored to God. True repentance includes my actions and attitudes (Phil. 2:5).

(3) Ask – Jesus taught us that we can *ask* of God. Paul gave us a great prayer list in Colossians 1:9-12. The spiritual nature of the prayers of Scriptures are helpful in praying for yourself and others.

(4) Yield – Jesus grew to the point where he could say, "not my will but yours be done." Yielding your desires (as hard as that may initially be) is an essential element of prayer. Once you've made known your requests, make sure you surrender your desires.

The 60 Minute Prayer Pattern:
The Hour that Changes the World

The Hour that Changes the World by Dick Eastman is a helpful pattern for increasing your time in prayer. Eastman divides 60 minutes into 12 periods of five minutes each to comprise an hour of prayer.

(1) Praise: *Recognize God's Nature* (Ps. 63:3).

(2) Waiting: *Silent Soul Surrender* (Ps. 46:10)

(3) Confession: *Temple Cleansing Time* (Ps. 139:23)

(4) Scripture Praying: *Word Enriched Prayer* (Jer. 23:29)

(5) Watching: *Develop Holy Alertness* (Col. 4:2)

(6) Intercession: *Remember the World* (1 Tim. 2:1-2)

(7) Petition: *Share Personal Needs* (Matt. 7:7)

(8) Thanksgiving: *Confess my Blessings* (1 Thes. 5:18)

(9) Singing: *Worship in Song* (Ps. 100:2)

(10) Meditation: *Ponder Spiritual Themes* (Josh 1:8)

(11) Listening: *Receive Spiritual Instruction* (Ecc. 5:2)

(12) Praise: *Recognize God's Nature* (Ps. 52:9)

Taken from *The Hour that Changes the World*[142]

Reflecting on the Character of God

Praise is an essential part of prayer. An abridged listing of the attributes and names of God follows. Reflecting upon one or two of these characteristics of God will enhance your prayer time.

Able – 2 Tim. 1:12

All Knowing – Psa. 139:1-6

Awesome – Neh. 1:5

Comforter – John 15:26

Conqueror – Rom. 8:35-39

Creator – Gen. 1

Defender – Zech. 9:15

Deliverer – Psalm 18:2

Everlasting Strength– Is. 9:6

Faithful – 1 Cor. 10:13

Forgiving – Psa. 130:4

Friend – Jn. 15:12-16

Glory – Psa. 24:7

God of Hope – Rom. 15:13

Gracious – Psa. 145:8

Great – Dan. 2:45

Guide – Psa. 23:3

Helper – Psa. 46:1

Hiding Place – Psa. 32:7

Holy – Isa. 6:3

Immortal – 1 Tim. 1:17

Infinite – Psa. 147:5

Jealous – Ex. 34:14

Just – Deut. 32:4

King – 1 Tim. 1:17

King of Kings – Rev. 19:16

Lamb of God – Jn. 1:29

Life – Jn. 14:6

Light – Jn. 8:12

Living God – Deut. 5:26

Lord of lords – Rev. 19:16

Love – Rom. 5:8

Majestic – 2 Pet. 1:17

Merciful – Psa. 86:15

Mighty God – Isa. 9:6

Mighty in battle – Psa. 24:8

Most high – Dan. 4:17

Near – Psa. 145:18-21

Omnipresent – Psa. 139:7,8

Omniscient – Psa. 139:1-6

Omnipotent – Job 42:2

Patient – 2 Pet. 3:9

Prince of Peace – Isa. 9:6

Protector – 2 Thes. 3:3

Provider – Heb. 11:40

Redeemer – Job 19:25

Refuge – Psa. 46:1

Rock – Psa. 18:1-2

Savior – Lk. 2:11

Shelter – Psa. 61:4

Strength – Psa. 28:7

Trustworthy–Psa. 84:10-12

Truth – Jn. 8:32, 14:6

Unchanging – Heb. 13:8

Unconquerable – Job 42:2

Victorious – 1 Cor. 15:57

Worthy – Revelation 5:12

From *God's Rx: Alphabet Soup* [143]

Bible Reading Schedule: A key chapter a day

It only takes a few minutes to read a chapter of the Bible. If you have never developed the habit of reading the Bible daily this is a great place to begin. If you already have a devotional pattern but would like to supplement it with additional Bible reading, consider using the following list. For additional Bible reading schedules and study tools visit www.biblicalstrategies.com.

Genesis 1	Exodus 10	Judges 7
Genesis 3	Exodus 11	Judges 14
Genesis 4	Exodus 12	Judges 15
Genesis 6	Exodus 13	Judges 16
Genesis 7	Exodus 14	Ruth 1
Genesis 8	Exodus 19	Ruth 2
Genesis 9	Exodus 20	Ruth 3
Genesis 11	Exodus 32	Ruth 4
Genesis 12	Leviticus 16	I Samuel 1
Genesis 15	Numbers 13	I Samuel 2
Genesis 18	Numbers 14	I Samuel 3
Genesis 21	Deuteronomy 1	I Samuel 8
Genesis 22	Deuteronomy 2	I Samuel 9
Genesis 24	Deuteronomy 3	I Samuel 10
Genesis 27	Deuteronomy 4	I Samuel 15
Genesis 28	Deuteronomy 5	I Samuel 16
Genesis 37	Deuteronomy 6	I Samuel 17
Genesis 39	Deuteronomy 7	2 Samuel 5
Genesis 40	Deuteronomy 8	2 Samuel 7
Genesis 41	Deuteronomy 27	2 Samuel 11
Genesis 42	Deuteronomy 28	2 Samuel 12
Genesis 43	Deuteronomy 29	I Kings 1
Genesis 44	Deuteronomy 30	I Kings 2
Genesis 45	Deuteronomy 32	I Kings 3
Genesis 50	Deuteronomy 34	I Kings 8
Exodus 1	Joshua 1	I Kings 9
Exodus 2	Joshua 2	I Kings 10
Exodus 3	Joshua 3	I Kings 11
Exodus 4	Joshua 4	I Kings 12
Exodus 5	Joshua 6	I Kings 17
Exodus 6	Joshua 23	I Kings 18
Exodus 7	Joshua 24	I Kings 19
Exodus 8	Judges 2	2 Kings 1
Exodus 9	Judges 6	2 Kings 2

2 Kings 4	Psalm 37	Amos 2
2 Kings 5	Psalm 90	Amos 9
2 Kings 6	Psalm 100	Obadiah
2 Kings 7	Psalm 103	Jonah 1
2 Kings 8	Psalm 104	Jonah 2
2 Kings 18	Psalm 105	Jonah 3
2 Kings 19	Psalm 106	Jonah 4
2 Kings 20	Psalm 107	Micah 5
2 Kings 25	Psalm 145	Micah 7
I Chronicles 17	Proverbs 1	Nahum 1
I Chronicles 29	Proverbs 2	Habakkuk 3
2 Chronicles 34	Proverbs 3	Zephaniah 3
2 Chronicles 35	Proverbs 4	Haggai 1
Ezra 1	Proverbs 5	Haggai 2
Ezra 3	Proverbs 6	Zechariah 14
Ezra 4	Proverbs 7	Malachi 3
Ezra 5	Proverbs 8	Malachi 4
Ezra 6	Proverbs 9	Matthew 5
Nehemiah 1	Proverbs 31	Matthew 6
Nehemiah 2	Ecclesiastes 3	Matthew 7
Nehemiah 4	Ecclesiastes 12	Matthew 13
Nehemiah 5	Song of Sol. 1	Matthew 17
Nehemiah 6	Isaiah 6	Matthew 21
Nehemiah 8	Isaiah 40	Matthew 24
Nehemiah 9	Isaiah 53	Matthew 25
Esther 1	Isaiah 55	Matthew 26
Esther 2	Isaiah 61	Matthew 27
Esther 3	Jeremiah 18	Matthew 28
Esther 4	Jeremiah 19	Mark 6
Esther 5	Jeremiah 31	Mark 8
Esther 6	Lamentations 3	Luke 1
Esther 7	Ezekiel 1	Luke 2
Esther 8	Ezekiel 37	Luke 4
Esther 9	Daniel 1	Luke 7
Job 1	Daniel 2	Luke 15
Job 2	Daniel 3	Luke 16
Job 38	Daniel 4	Luke 18
Job 39	Daniel 5	Luke 19
Job 40	Daniel 6	Luke 20
Job 41	Daniel 9	Luke 24
Job 42	Hosea 4	John 1
Psalm 1	Hosea 14	John 3
Psalm 19	Joel 2	John 4
Psalm 23	Amos 1	John 6

John 8	1 Corinthians 7	2 Timothy 4
John 10	1 Corinthians 8	Titus 1
John 13	1 Corinthians 9	Titus 2
John 14	1 Corinthians 13	Titus 3
John 15	1 Corinthians 15	Philemon
John 16	2 Corinthians 1	Hebrews 1
John 17	2 Corinthians 4	Hebrews 2
John 20	2 Corinthians 5	Hebrews 4
John 21	2 Corinthians 8	Hebrews 8
Acts 1	2 Corinthians 9	Hebrews 9
Acts 2	2 Corinthians 12	Hebrews 11
Acts 7	Galatians 5	Hebrews 12
Acts 8	Galatians 6	Hebrews 13
Acts 9	Ephesians 1	James 1
Acts 10	Ephesians 2	James 2
Acts 13	Ephesians 3	James 3
Acts 15	Ephesians 4	James 4
Acts 16	Ephesians 5	James 5
Acts 17	Ephesians 6	1 Peter 1
Acts 18	Philippians 1	1 Peter 2
Acts 21	Philippians 2	1 Peter 3
Acts 22	Philippians 3	1 Peter 4
Acts 23	Philippians 4	1 Peter 5
Acts 24	Colossians 1	2 Peter 1
Acts 25	Colossians 2	2 Peter 2
Acts 26	Colossians 3	2 Peter 3
Acts 27	Colossians 4	1 John 1
Acts 28	1 Thessalonians 1	1 John 2
Romans 1	1 Thessalonians 2	1 John 3
Romans 2	1 Thessalonians 3	1 John 4
Romans 3	1 Thessalonians 4	1 John 5
Romans 4	1 Thessalonians 5	2 John
Romans 5	2 Thessalonians 1	3 John
Romans 6	2 Thessalonians 2	Jude
Romans 7	2 Thessalonians 3	Revelation 1
Romans 8	1 Timothy 1	Revelation 2
Romans 12	1 Timothy 2	Revelation 3
Romans 13	1 Timothy 3	Revelation 4
Romans 14	1 Timothy 4	Revelation 5
Romans 15	1 Timothy 5	Revelation 19
1 Corinthians 1	1 Timothy 6	Revelation 20
1 Corinthians 2	2 Timothy 1	Revelation 21
1 Corinthians 3	2 Timothy 2	Revelation 22
1 Corinthians 6	2 Timothy 3	

Taken from *Drawing Near* [144]

3 Questions of Bible Study

(1) Observation asks, "What do I see?" Observation is simply gathering all the facts of who, what, where, and when. Careful examination of the facts is the foundation upon which we build accurate interpretation . . . The more time spent looking at the text itself, reading and rereading it, the more fruitful our study will be.

(2) Interpretation asks, "What does it mean?" Drawing conclusions based on your study of the facts is the process of interpretation . . . we seek to understand the meaning that the author had in mind.

(3) Application asks, "How should I respond?" Application is the goal of Bible Study. It is not enough for us to understand (interpret) Scripture; God wants us to be changed by it. In this final step of the inductive process, we move from the original context to our contemporary one, seeking to know how our interpretation can affect our attitudes and behavior.

Taken from *Unlocking the Scriptures* [145]

9 Questions for Application

- Is there an example for me to follow?
- Is there a sin to avoid?
- Is there a promise to claim?
- Is there a prayer to repeat?
- Is there a command to obey?
- Is there a condition to meet?
- Is there a verse to memorize?
- Is there an error to mark?
- Is there a challenge to face?

Taken from *Living by the Book* [146]

Next Steps to Change

(1) Set short-term goals – Are there short-term goals I need to accomplish this change?

(2) Pray specifically – What specific ways do I need to pray for change? With whom can I share these prayer requests?

(3) Search biblical resources – Are there other biblical resources that would help me change (i.e. books, media, websites, etc)?

(4) Develop a long-term plan – Is there a long term plan I need to put in place as I move towards changing?

(5) Acquire accountability – Would I benefit from an accountability partner? Who will it be? When will I contact him/her?

4 Helpful Tools for Bible Study

(1) A Study Bible – Study Bibles provide helpful book introductions, background information, and interpretive notes. They typically focus on knowledge *or* application. Of the first category, I recommend: *The ESV Study Bible* and *The MacArthur Study Bible*. For application I recommend *The Life Application Bible* and *The Life Essentials Study Bible*.

(2) Cross Referencing Tools – Your Bible may have some cross references in the margin. If you wish to do a more extended study, I recommend *The Treasury of Scripture Knowledge*. Multiple references are available when you look up your passage of choice.

(3) Word Studies – Reference tools that will tap the original language and original meaning of the words are beneficial in the discovery process. I recommend *Vine's Expository Dictionary of New Testament and Old Testament*

Words and *The Key Word Study Bible* by Spiros Zodhiates.

4) Book Summaries and Outlines – Understanding the purpose of the writer and the flow of the particular book in the Bible are important for setting the context. I recommend *How to Read the Bible Book by Book* by Gordon Fee and Douglas Stuart.

The Scripture Retrieval Method

The Scripture retrieval method is based upon three premises: (1) Scripture provides an excellent *defense* against temptation. This is why the first 10 verses listed below are learned in the lie/truth formula to defend against temptation (2) Scripture provides an excellent *offense* to weaken temptation's appeal. This is why the second 10 verses are learned about the character of God and the nature of the Gospel. Loving God well and appreciating the Gospel weakens the draw of temptation. (3) We learn the Scriptures best when we *understand* the words we are memorizing and *apply* them to our real life challenges. For this reason, rote memory is ineffective as a means of defending against sin.

Biblical Truths to Combat the Deceiver's Lies

Lie 1: No one will ever know what you are about to do. Go ahead. No one is watching. Truth: Hebrews 4:13

Lie 2: This temptation is too difficult. Go ahead give in. Truth: 1 Corinthians 10:13

Lie 3: You keep failing. You'll never have victory over this sin. Truth: Philippians 1:6; 4:13

Lie 4: Your past is too bad. You can't overcome it. Truth: Philippians 3:13-14

Lie 5: You can't change. That's just the way you are. Truth: 2 Corinthians 5:17

Lie 6: God is keeping something good from you.
Truth: Psalm 84:10-12

Lie 7: You can avoid the consequences. Your situation is unique. Truth: Job 31:11-12 NLT; Galatians 6:7-9

Lie 8: The temptation is so strong God must want you to sin.
Truth: James 1:13-15

Lie 9: You can overcome this sin alone. Don't tell anybody.
Truth: James 5:16; Psalm 32:3-5

Lie 10: If it feels right it must be right.
Truth: Ephesians 4:22-24

Biblical Promises about God and the Gospel

Promise 1: God is good, loving, and faithful.
Passage: Psalm 100:5

Promise 2: God loves me and enjoys acting on my behalf.
Passage: Zephaniah 3:17

Promise 3: God sacrificed his Son to show his love for me
Truth: Romans 5:8, 10

Promise 4: Nothing can separate me from the love of   God.
Passage: Romans 8:35, 37

Promise 5: God is purposefully at work in my life and circumstances. Passage: Jeremiah 29:11, 13

Promise 6: God will never stop loving me.
Passage: Lamentations 3:23-24

Promise 7: God will always be with me.
Passage: Hebrews 13:6

Promise 8: God is near when I'm in trouble.
Passage: Psalm 46:1-2

Promise 9: Having been forgiven, I need not fear God's condemnation. Passage: Romans 8:1

Promise 10: God saved me because of who he is, not because of who I am. Passage: Titus 3:4-6

Visit www.biblicalstrategies.com to order these 20 memory verse cards with helpful commentary on the back of each card

The Blind Runner Reflection

Reread the story of the blind runner (page 50) Reflect upon that image. Imagine the trust he must place in those who are leading him. Does this picture adequately portray your dependence upon the Holy Spirit? Why or why not? Are you moving forward under the Holy Spirit's direction? Are you sensitive to his leading? Would those who know you best give the same answer?

The TRUST Acrostic

Many Christians are unfamiliar with the work of the Holy Spirit, and even less certain with how to apply his work in their lives. As we mature in Christ, we should grow in our *dependence* upon the Holy Spirit. I use the word TRUST to underscore my interaction with the Spirit of God. I encourage you to memorize the acrostic and reflect upon it daily. Choose one key area that needs further development and give that special attention.

Turn to Him when you're hurting (John 14:16, 17).
Rely upon Him when you're weary (Rom. 8:26-27).
Understand the Word with His help (Jn. 16:13).
Submit, even when you don't understand (Mark 1:12).
Terminate old decision-making habits (Gal. 5:16, 18).

(1) Turn to Him when you're hurting (John 14:16, 17). Jesus promised the Holy Spirit to the disciples during a time when they were troubled and their future was uncertain (John 14:1). The Holy Spirit is described as the comforter who will come along side. Because he dwells with us *and* in us, we are never alone.

(2) Rely upon Him when you're weary (Rom. 8:26-27). When we are weak, the Spirit helps us. When we are uncertain on how to pray, the Spirit steps in. When

our emotional pain seems to take our breath away, the Spirit is interceding on our behalf. Most importantly, the Spirit does all this for us in accordance with the will of God.

(3) Understand the Word with His help (Jn. 16:13). While this promise was given to the disciples, it has a broader application to the rest of believers. The Holy Spirit is sent by the Father to be our guide and to lead us (Rom. 8:14; Gal. 5:18). Be willing to receive the Spirit's assistance when you open the Word.

(4) Submit, even when you don't understand (Mark 1:12). Mark 1:12 states that the Spirit *drove* Jesus into the wilderness to be tempted. Jesus may not have chosen this location or venue to be tested, but he willingly submitted to the Spirit in it. Our tendency will be to lean into our flesh when we don't understand (Gal. 5:17). We are challenged to keep in step with the Spirit (Gal. 5:25 NIV). Unexplainable difficulties provide an excellent opportunity for us to submit to a Spirit-filled response.

(5) Terminate old decision-making habits (Gal. 5:16, 18). We are introduced to the fruit of the Spirit (Gal. 5:22, 23) *after* a listing of the deeds of our flesh (Gal. 5:19-21). The context is significant. Our greatest success in overcoming sinful habits will be to embrace new habits. As we take off our past ways of thinking, we are to put on God's ways. We terminate the old and we put on the new.

Tool Box Analogy for the Fruit of the Spirit

Consider the *Fruit of the Spirit* like a toolbox. Inside are tools for every situation. You wouldn't use a hammer to do the job of screwdriver, nor would you attempt to saw a board with a wrench. Likewise, when you enter into challenging relationships and situations, choose the part of the fruit that is most effective for that difficulty. To do so, you will need to learn the fruit and practice it. Only then will you become proficient in its application. I have included my working definitions of each part of the fruit of the Spirit. You can use these or develop your own through reflection and Bible study. Working with the given definitions, make a list of the various relationships you encounter and prayerfully consider which tool best suits the challenge in that relationship. For example, perhaps you need patience with your kids, mercy with your spouse, and love with your fellow employee. Keep those ideas in the forefront of your mind as you engage in that particular relational challenge. If your children are disrespectful, ask yourself how you can best demonstrate patience in this context. Now depend upon the Holy Spirit's leading to enable you to do so.

- Love is a sacrificial choice (1 Jn. 3:16) of words accompanied by actions (1 Jn. 3:18) regardless of attraction or response (Rom. 5:8) generated by God not by oneself (Jn. 21:15-18).

- Joy is a pre-determined attitude (Phil. 4:4) of praise for God's goodness (Psa. 5:11) by maintaining an eternal focus (Psa. 16:11) in the midst of difficulty (Heb. 12:2).

- Peace is a settled confidence of mind (Phil. 4:7) from a right relationship with God (Phil. 4:9) unaffected by circumstantial change (4:11).

- Patience is a learned attitude (Col. 1:11) revealed through a joyful willingness (Jam. 1:2) to remain under difficulty (Jam. 1:3-4) in order to learn God's lessons (Jam. 5:11).

- Kindness is a tender spirit purposefully expressed (Rom 2:4) sacrificially given (Eph 2:7), especially to the undeserving (Titus 3:4).

- Goodness is focused resolve (2 Thes. 1:11) that drives us to become actively involved in the life of another (2 Chron. 24:16), consistently expressed through generosity (Neh. 9:25).

- Faithfulness is a promise (Rom. 3:3; Lam. 3:23) to keep one's word and do one's best (1 Th. 1:3) with a servant-attitude focused on the Master's approval (Matt 25:21).

- Gentleness is an attitude of humility (Jam. 1:21) stirred by grateful spirit (Num. 12:3; Ps. 90:15) revealed in a tenderness to others (Eph. 4:2) sustained by a growing trust in God (Matt. 5:5).

- Self-control is the growing realization that one's desire to please self was crucified with Christ and replaced with a desire to glorify God (Gal. 2:20).

NOTES

1. The narrative is my imaginative retelling of the birth of Jesus. Where I have referenced the Scriptures (like Joseph naming Jesus), the narrative is historically accurate. Where there is no biblical reference (like Joseph humming Mary's song), I believe it to be a reasonable consideration.

2. Genesis 3:16

3. Galatians 4:4

4. Matthew 1:22, 25

5. John 1:14

6. John 1:14, 1 John 4:2

7. John 1:1-4

8. 1 John 2:6

9. Matthew 10:38

10. I was first introduced to the phrase "the intrinsic limitations of humanity" through the teaching of Dr. Doug Bookman. Bookman is a New Testament scholar whose career has been spent studying the life of Christ. Most Christians understand that Jesus lived with the intrinsic limitations of humanity *physically* (i.e. he needed sleep, nourishment, and shelter), but the Bible also communicates that Jesus lived within those same limits *spiritually*. The Scriptures tell us that he endured life's hardships and learned through them (Heb. 5:8), that he grew in favor with God and man despite the latter's sinfulness and imperfect treatment of him throughout his life (Luke 2:48; 4:29; 23:20-25), and that while he lived and was tempted within those human limitations, he never sinned (Heb. 4:15; 1 John 3: 5; 4:2).

11. Hebrews 4:15

12. Bookman writes "And the Scriptures make clear that *Jesus' humanity was genuine and entire.* Thus, as we read the Gospel narratives of Jesus' life it is important to remember that except at those occasional and relatively infrequent times when the Holy Spirit directed Jesus to access and employ the superhuman capacities which are a function of His divine attributes, *He lived out His life under the actual and real limitations intrinsic to humanity*" (emphasis added). So how could Jesus remain fully God and yet still operate within humanity's limitations? The answer, in part, is found in the phrase "emptied himself" (*kenosis*) used in Philippians 2:7. Paul describes the incarnation (God becoming man) this way: "who, although He existed in the form of God, did not regard equality with God a thing to be grasped, but *emptied Himself*, taking the form of a bond-servant, and being made in the likeness of men." Perhaps the best understanding of this phrase is that Jesus *voluntarily surrendered the independent use of his divine attributes.* He did not stop being God, but now, he would wait on the Holy Spirit to direct him and empower him in the use of those attributes. *He would operate within the intrinsic limitations of humanity.* Secondly, he would not use these attributes for his personal gain or glory, but only for the Father's.

13. Mark 1:35

14. This narrative is my imaginative retelling of the morning prayer of Jesus. The historical record is found in Mark 1:29-39.

15. Matthew 14:23-25; Mark 1:35; 6:46; Luke 6:12

16. Mark 1:34

17. Mark 1:24-26

18. Mark 1:27, 28, 45; 2:12; 3:7-11

19. Mark 1:10, 12, 18, 20, 23, 29, 30

20. Mark 1:35-38 NKJV

21. J. Oswald Sanders, *Spiritual Leadership* (Chicago, IL: Moody Press, 1994), 86.

22. Mark 1:35, Luke 6:12

23. Mark 1:35

24. Exodus 24:4, 34:4

25. Job 1:5

26. Nehemiah 8:3

27. Mark 1:35 NKJV

28. W.E. Vine, *Vine's Expository Dictionary of New Testament Words* (McLean, VA: MacDonald Publishing, 1989), 299.

29. Philippians 4:8

30. Mark 1:35, 38

31. Matthew 4:13

32. Mark 1:37

33. Mark 1:38

34. Mark 1:35

35. Luke 6:12-13

36. God the Father spoke to, or on behalf of the Son, from heaven in an audible voice three times: at his baptism (Matt. 3:17), when he was transfigured (Mark 9:7), and during the final week of his life when his soul was troubled (John 12:28). This is significant. The Father's response to Jesus' prayer time does not appear to be all that different from when you and I pray.

37. Luke 2:40, 52

38. Matthew 6:9-14

39. Luke 6:12

40. Matthew 26:40

41. In the final six months of Jesus' ministry, he makes three trips to the Jerusalem area for the Feast of Booths (John 7:20), Feast of Dedication (John 10:22), and the raising of Lazarus (Luke 11:1-44). As the first two follow Hebrew calendared events, we can date his teaching about prayer for the disciples (Luke 11:1-4) to within months of their attempt to pray with him in the Garden of Gethsemane.

42. Isaiah 55:8, 9

43. Romans 1:9-20

44. Job 38-41

45. In our English Bibles, whenever the name "Lord" is written with all capital letters (LORD), it signifies the translation of the Hebrew name "Yahweh," the name used to declare the covenant keeping character of God.

46. Nehemiah 1:5

47. Nancy Adels, *God's RX: Alphabet Soup* (Maitland, FL: Xulon Press, 2012).

48. Matthew 26:36-46

49. Hebrews 12:2

50. Matthew 26:36-46

51. Luke 2:51; 4:1; 7:6-10; 22:39-46; John 19:10-11

52. 2 Corinthians 12:7-10

53. 2 Corinthians 12:8

54. Ibid.

55. 2 Corinthians 12:9

56. 2 Corinthians 12:9-10

57. Matthew 4:4

58. Mark 1:13

59. Deuteronomy 8:2-3

60. John 17:1-5

61. John 17:6-19

62. John 17:20-26

63. John 18:1

64. The number of lambs slain at Passover (200,000 on one occasion) is recorded by the Jewish historian Josephus (Josephus VI.ix.3).

65. Mark 14:35

66. John MacArthur, *The MacArthur Study Bible* (Wheaton, IL: Crossway Books, 1997), 1561.

67. Luke 22:43 68 2 Corinthians 5:20

68. Matthew 17:20-21

69. Matthew 6:10

70. This narrative is my imaginative retelling of the temptation of Jesus. The historical record is found in Matthew 4:1-11, Mark 1:12-13, Luke 4:1-13.

71. Mark declares that the angels ministered to Jesus following his 40-day fast (Mark 1:13). This is significant. Only one other time do the gospel writers refer to angels ministering to Jesus (Luke 22:43). Undoubtedly, the 40-day fast had taken a severe toll on his physical body.

72. 1 Peter 5:8-9

73. Deuteronomy 8:3

74. Matthew 22:32-33

75. Matthew 4:4, 7, 10

76. Matthew 18:22

77. Luke 2:40, 52

78. Colossians 1:28

79. 2 Timothy 2:15

80. Howard Hendricks, *Living by the Book* (Chicago, IL: Moody Publishers, 1991), 166.

81. Elton Trueblood, *The New Man for our Time* (New York City, NY: Harper Collins, 1970).

82. James 1:22

83. James 4:17

84. Matthew 28:20 NLT

85. Exodus 15:26; Deuteronomy 6:3-5; Luke 6:47; 8:21; 11:28

86. Ken Ramey, *Expository Listening* (The Woodlands, TX: Kress Biblical Resources, 2010), 87, 94-95.

87. Matthew 23:2, 3

88. Ezra 7:10

89. www.scientificamerican.com/article.cfm?id=what-is-the-memory-capacity

90. 1 Corinthians 10:12-13

91. Philippians 2:8

92. Matthew 4:4, 7, 10

93. Genesis 3:5

94. Matthew 4:5

95. Jude 9

96. Isaiah 28:9-10

97. Matthew 4:1-11

98. Luke 4:13

99. www.cbssports.com/nfl/story/13350572/private-showing-ryans-road-to-qb-stardom-paved-with-tape

100. James 1:19-20

101. 1 John 2:16

102. Matthew 4:1-11; Luke 4:1-13

103. This narrative is my imaginative retelling of the baptism of Jesus. The historical record is found in Matthew 3:1-17, Mark 1:1-11, Luke 3:21-22.

104. John 1:23

105. John 3:13-15

106. Luke 3:21

107. Luke 3:21

108. Luke 3:22

109. Luke 4:1

110. Luke 4:1, 16

111. Luke 4:1

112. Luke 4:1

113. Spiros Zodhiates, *Hebrew Greek Key Study Bible* (Chattanooga, TN: AMG Publishers, 1986), 1721.

114. Acts 7:55

115. Luke 4:1

116. Ephesians 5:18

117. Luke 4:2, 6, 9

118. Luke 4:1

119. Galatians 5:16, 18, 25 NIV

120. John MacArthur, *Galatians* (Chicago, IL: Moody Press, 1987), 152.

121. Ephesians 5:15-16

122. Galatians 6:8-9

123. Galatians 6:9

124. Ephesians 2:2-3 NASV

125. Vine, *Vine's Expository Dictionary of New Testament Words*, 751.

126. Mark 10:44-45

127. 2 Corinthians 10:5; Philippians 4:8

128. Romans 12:2

129. Ephesians 2:10

130. Ephesians 4:17-19

131. Ephesians 2:10

132. Galatians 2:20

133. Galatians 1:10

134. Genesis 1: 10, 12, 21, 25

135. Matthew 4:1; Luke 4:1

136. Mark 1:12-13

137. Luke 4:1

138. Romans 8:14

139. Galatians 5:17, 18

140. Matthew 4:1; Luke 4:1

141. James 1:13

142. Dick Eastman, *The Hour That Changes the World* (Grand Rapids, MI: Chosen Books, 2002), 118.

143. Nancy Adels, *God's RX: Alphabet Soup*, 15-107.

144. Kenneth Boa and Max Anders, *Drawing Near* (Nashville, TN: Thomas Nelson Publishers, 1987), 117-120.

145. Hans Finzel, *Unlocking the Scriptures* (Colorado Springs, CO: Cook Publishers, 2003), 19.

146. Howard Hendricks, *Living by the Book*, 304-307.

About Biblical Strategies

A strategy is a plan of action designed to achieve a specific goal. Biblical strategies are unique in that they derive their foundation and plan from the Bible. God, being both mankind's creator and the Bible's author, is uniquely positioned to address the challenges we face. He knows us, and knows the best plan of action for our growth.

God has chosen to communicate this plan through the pages of Scripture. Through the Bible, we discover: our Father's plan of action, Jesus' godly example, and ways the Holy Spirit can empower us. Biblical strategies focus on select Scriptures, applying them to situations where we are prone to struggle.

- The *Biblical Strategies Booklet Series* is comprised of brief, 60-70 page booklets that provide biblical instruction and practical suggestions for applying the truths learned.

- The *Scripture Retrieval Method* is a unique approach to memorizing Biblical passages. A select set of 20 Bible verses are chosen for specific temptations. To expose the temptation's deception, we memorize ten verses in the lie/truth formula. To weaken the temptation's appeal, we learn ten promises about the character of God and the nature of the gospel. To aid understanding, we include biblical commentary on the back of each card.

- The website (biblicalstrategies.com) provides numerous resources, diagrams, plans and brief essays to strengthen your Christian walk. Most are available for free download.

About the Author

Phil Moser is the author of the Biblical Strategies Series. He is a pastor, frequent blogger (philmoser.com) and conference speaker. He holds a Bachelor of Science degree in Business Management, and earned his Masters of Divinity from The Master's Seminary, Sun Valley, California.

He presently serves as the teaching pastor of Fellowship Bible Church, Sewell, New Jersey. He has served as an adjunct professor teaching the Bible, theology, apologetics, homiletics, and counseling courses to undergraduate and graduate students in California, Florida, New York, Albania, Korea, Germany, Hungary and Ukraine.

He grew up in rural Indiana. His family moved to South Carolina during his teen years. He has been happily married to his wife, Kym, for 25 years. Together they have lived in California, New York and New Jersey; they have four children.

He loves discovering truths about God from the Bible, and finds joy in sharing those practical applications with others. He enjoys music (of nearly any genre), fly-fishing (even when they're not biting), and cheering for whichever Indiana team is playing basketball at the moment.

If you would like the author to speak to your group, you may contact him through the biblical strategies website.

Biblical Strategies
How you get to where God's taking you.
BiblicalStrategies.com